MY BOOK
OF HEROES

ISBN: 1729559751
ISBN-13: 978-1729559758

MCCAIN WAS "NOT A WAR HERO BECAUSE HE WAS
CAPTURED. I LIKE PEOPLE THAT WEREN'T CAPTURED.."

—DONALD TRUMP

REALITYJOURNALS.COM

www.ingramcontent.com/pod-product-compliance
Lightning Source LLC
Chambersburg PA
CBHW061324250726
48657CB00016B/325